PUFFIN BOOKS

# The Christmas Stocking Joke Book

Every aspect of the festive season, from turkey and stuffing to Santa and his reindeer, is included in this side-splitting new collection of lively Christmas jokes and cartoons. You'll still be laughing well into the New Year!

Anyone wanting to give their ribs a rest had better watch out, because there's something here to rouse even Uncle George from his post-pudding slumbers.

Shoo Rayner is a highly original author/illustrator of several picture books. This is his first joke book for older children. Shoo Rayner lives and works in Wales.

for Georgina

Shoo Rayner

# The Christmas Stocking Joke Book

PUFFIN BOOKS

PUFFIN BOOKS

Published by the Penguin Group
27 Wrights Lane, London W8 5TZ, England
Viking Penguin Inc., 40 West 23rd Street, New York,
New York 10010, USA
Penguin Books Australia Ltd, Ringwood, Victoria, Australia
Penguin Books Canada Ltd, 2801 John Street, Markham, Ontario,
Canada L3R 1B4
Penguin Books (NZ) Ltd, 182–190 Wairau Road, Auckland 10, New Zealand

Penguin Books Ltd, Registered Offices: Harmondsworth,
Middlesex, England

First published 1989
3 5 7 9 10 8 6 4 2

Copyright © Shoo Rayner, 1989
All rights reserved

Filmset in Linotron Oldstyle No. 7 by
Rowland Phototypesetting Ltd, Bury St Edmunds, Suffolk
Printed in Great Britain by Cox and Wyman Ltd, Reading, Berks.

# Santa Banter

Santa is very clever.
He passed his
diplohohoma.

Who says Oh Oh Oh?
*Santa walking backwards.*

One Christmas Eve a policeman found a
man on the pavement who had been knocked
over.
'Did you get the car's registration number?'
asked the policeman.
'No,' said the man, 'but I'd recognize those
reindeer anywhere!'

What did Santa say
to the little chimney?

You're too young to smoke.

How many chimneys
does Santa have to climb
down on Christmas Eve?

Stacks!

Not much on telly this Christmas!

Why does Santa wear underpants?
*Because he used to be called Saint Knickerless.*

What did the reindeer say to Santa when he told him a joke?
*'This one will sleigh you.'*

What's this thing?

It's the North Pole.

NORTH POLE

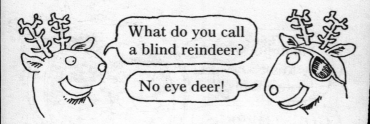

What do you call a blind reindeer?

No eye deer!

Why does Santa wear bright red braces?
*To hold his trousers up of course.*

The Three Wise Men's wise fronts!

Tina always put a great big arrow next to her house so that Santa wouldn't forget to visit.
'But he always comes,' said Tina's mum.
'I know,' said Tina. 'It works every time.'

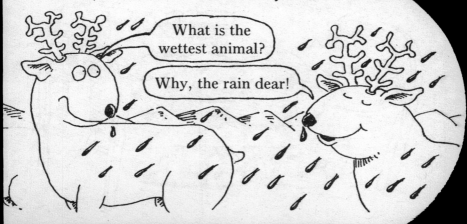

What is the wettest animal?

Why, the rain dear!

Santa knows we're suckers for one thing GOBSTOPPERS.

Did you hear about the twin brothers who were so close that they hung up a pair of tights for Santa?

Jim used to be frightened of Santa and used to hide under the bed . . . mind you, he was always a little potty.

Stupid boy!

When Santa got to England he got stuck in a chimney.

Now he's the toast of London!

Tina was so excited on Christmas Eve, she just couldn't get to sleep. Mum said, 'Sleep on the side of the bed, you'll soon drop off.'

# CRACKER

Why did the chicken cross the road?
*Because it wanted to see a man laying bricks.*

Which animals use nut crackers?
*Toothless squirrels.*

Did you hear about the mad scientist who invented the waterproof teabag?

I thought you were going to come round and fix the doorbell yesterday.
*I did – I rang twice but you didn't answer!*

t would you call Batman and Robin if
had been run over by a steamroller?
*nan and Ribbon.*

# JOKES

Why didn't the millionaire have any bathrooms in his mansion?
*Because he was filthy rich.*

How do you keep an idiot in suspense?
*I'll tell you tomorrow!*

What kind of dog does a hairdresser have?
*A shampoodle.*

What happened to the karate expert when he joined the army?
*He knocked himself out when he saluted.*

What do you give a man who can't get into a pair of trousers?
*A kilt.*

# Seasonings

'Eat up your sprouts, dear, and you'll grow
up to be very pretty.'
*'Oh dear, didn't you eat sprouts when you
were young, Gran?'*

'You just don't appreciate good food.'
*'I would if you ever cooked any.'*

'I've just eaten the wishbone.'
*'Are you choking?'*
'No, I'm deadly serious!'

'Tina, there were six mince pies in this tin
last night. Why is there only one now?'
*'Well, it was so dark I thought there were
only five!'*

We always say prayers before we eat . . .
Mum's a terrible cook.

'Don't eat off your knife, Jim.'
*'But, Dad, my fork leaks.'*

We had chips for Christmas lunch . . .
Christmas was on a Friday this year.

Dad said it would be best if Mum didn't eat
over Christmas . . . Mum said that she'd
rather have second best, thank you!

'These are the best mince pies I've made in
years.'
*'Then it's time you got a new recipe.'*

What do monsters like to eat for Christmas?
*Kate and Sydney pie.*

Excuse me . . .
Did you know that
you've got mince pies
stuck in your ears?

Sorry . . .
I can't hear you –
I've got mince pies
stuck in my ears!

We had Australian Christmas puddings. We tried to throw them away but they kept coming back. They were Boo Meringues!

We had duck instead of turkey for Christmas. It was a quistmas quacker!

QUACK

QUACK

Why aren't elves allowed their Christmas lunch?
*Because they're always goblin their food.*

Hi ho, Hi ho,

It's gobble, gobble, gobble we go!

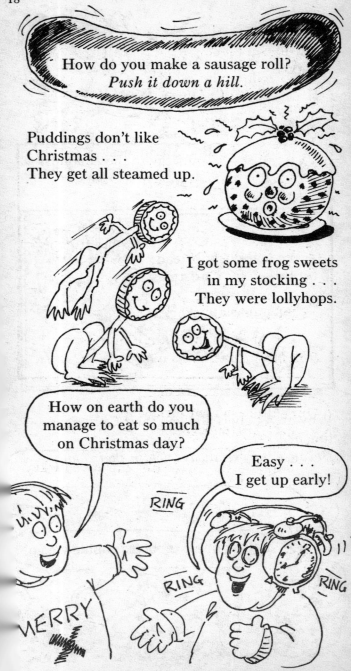

How do you make a sausage roll?
*Push it down a hill.*

Puddings don't like
Christmas . . .
They get all steamed up.

I got some frog sweets
in my stocking . . .
They were lollyhops.

How on earth do you
manage to eat so much
on Christmas day?

Easy . . .
I get up early!

How do you make
an apple crumble?
*Hit it with a hammer.*

SPLAT.

What did the biscuits say to the almonds?
*You're nuts and we're crackers.*

Name me three kinds of nuts.
*Hazelnuts, brazil nuts and forget-me-nuts.*

Our cat doesn't eat turkey
on Christmas Day.

But cats love turkey.

I know, we just
don't give it any!

MEANIES!

A TELLING TAIL!

# CRACKER

What did the first doctor say to the other doctor?
*You look well, how am I?*

What do you get if you dial 29467924217465864830?
*A blister on your finger.*

What grows in a field and makes music?
*Pop corn.*

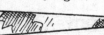

Did you hear about the man who always had aeroplanes outside his house?
He used to leave the landing lights on.

What happened to the man who stole a calendar?
*He got twelve months.*

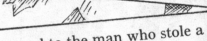

# JOKES

What lives at the bottom of the sea, has eight wheels and carries people around?
*An octobus.*

What do you give a hungry robber?
*Beefburglers.*

Doctor, doctor, I think I've lost my memory.
*When did you find out?*
Find out what?

What is green, red and hairy?
*A gooseberry with nappy rash.*

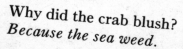

Why did the crab blush?
*Because the sea weed.*

# Just What I Always Wanted

Jim got a brand-new bicycle for Christmas.
As he whizzed down the hill he called out,
'Look, Tina, no hands!'
As the bike picked up speed he called out,
'Look, Tina, no feet!'
As he crashed into the back of a lorry he called,
'Noook, Ina, no teef!'

'Dad, Jim's broken my new doll.'
*'How did he do that?'*
'I hit him on the head with it!'

Mum wanted a car for Christmas.
Dad gave her a great big ball
of steel wool and told her
to knit one!

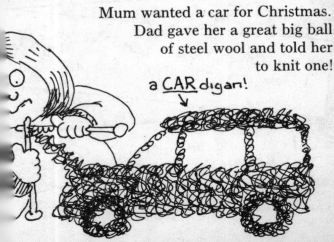

a CAR digan!

'I was given a wombat for Christmas.'
*'What do you do with a wombat?'*
'I hit woms with it, stupid!'

I got a bottle of whiskey for my dad.

Well, that sounds like a good deal!

Last year I gave
my baby brother
measles for Christmas!

gloop
gloop
gloop

'What's two foot long, has a hundred hairy
legs and goes GLOOP, GLOOP, GLOOP?'
*'I don't know, what's two foot long, has a
hundred hairy legs and goes GLOOP,
GLOOP, GLOOP?'*
'I don't know either, but that's what you're
getting for Christmas!'

Granny gave me a present
to help me stop biting
my nails . . .
It was a pair of shoes.

Grandad really suffers
from wind, so we gave
him a kite for Christmas.

Grandad was in a shop looking at train se
'Your grandson would love to have a set li
that one,' said the salesman.
'You're absolutely right,' said Grandad.
'In that case, I'd better have two sets!'

What do you give the man
who has everything for
Christmas?
*Penicillin.*

What do you give
a railway station
master for
Christmas?
*Platform shoes,
of course!*

I got a portable
for Christmas.

A portable what?

I'm not sure really –
I've only got the
handle so far!

Dad bought Mum a belt
for Christmas.
It's like a dustcart . . . .
It goes round gathering
up the waist.

I sewed two stockings together
but I didn't get any more presents.
It must have been a TIGHT fit.

Guess what our builder gave
his wife for Christmas?
*A ladder in her stocking.*

Auntie Astrid got a new fur coat for
Christmas. I don't know what it's made of,
but every time she walks past a dog the fur
stands up on her back.

I wouldn't mind a
coat like that!

# DING DONG BELL

Knock, knock.
*Who's there?*
Don.
*Don who?*
Don mess about,
open the door!

Knock, knock.
*Who's there?*
Jemima.
*Jemima who?*
Jemima asking
who lives here?

Knock, knock.
*Who's there?*
Harry.
*Harry who?*
Harry up and
open the door.

Knock, knock.
*Who's there?*
Godfrey.
*Godfrey who?*
Godfrey tickets
to the pantomime.

Knock, knock.
*Who's there?*
Boo.
*Boo who?*
Don't cry, it's
only a joke!

It's cold
out here

MILK

# CRACKER

Why is a hotdog the noblest dog of all?
*Because it feeds the hand that bites it.*

What did the chicken say to the orange?
*Look what marmalade.*

What are long, horny, twisted and dirty?
*Your toenails!*

What is yellow and very good at adding up?
*A banana with a calculator.*

How many ears does Mr Spock have?
*A left ear, a right ear and a final frontier.*

# JOKES

What happened to the mathematician who got his head stuck in the railings?
*He had to work it out with a pencil.*

Why isn't your head twelve inches wide?
*Because then it would be a foot.*

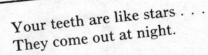

What do you call a flying policeman?
*A helicopper.*

Your teeth are like stars . . .
They come out at night.

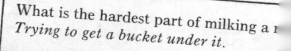

What is the hardest part of milking a r
*Trying to get a bucket under it.*

# SNOWMAN'S LAND

Where did Mr and
Mrs Snowman meet?
*At the Snow Ball.*

What do they sing at a snowman's birthday
party?
*Freeze a jolly good fellow.*

Why is it difficult to keep a
secret at the North Pole?
*Because your teeth tend to chatter.*

'Why is your house so cold?'
*'Because Dad doesn't know the difference
between toothpaste and putty.'*
'What on earth has that got to do with it?'
*'Well, all the window panes keep falling out.'*

Tina! If you break
your legs on that toboggan,
don't come running to me!

Jim, I told you
to share your new
sledge with Tina.

I did. I had it on
the way down and Tina
had it on the way up!

What's white, furry and smells of peppermint?
*A POLO bear.*

Where would you find a polar bear?
*I didn't know one was lost.*

What do polar bears eat?
*Ice burgers.*

Why shouldn't you take a polar bear to the zoo?

Because he'd rather go to the funfair.

What is an ig?
*An Eskimo's house without a loo.*

How does an Eskimo make his house?
*Igloos it together.*

If your mum comes from Iceland and your
dad comes from Cuba then what are you?
*An Ice Cube.*

What kind of money do Eskimos use?
*Iced lolly.*

Why do Eskimos eat candles?
*For a little light refreshment.*

Two Eskimos were talking about their dogs.
'That one's barking his head off,' said one of
the Eskimos.
'I know,' said the other, 'it's making him a
little husky!'

One Eskimo asked another where his mother
came from. 'Alaska,' was his reply.
'Oh, never mind,' said his friend, 'I'll ask her
myself!'

An Eskimo mum had twins . . .
They were blubber and sister!

A young Eskimo boy was late for school one
morning. When the teacher asked him why
he was late he said,
'Well, it's so icy outside that for every step I
took forward I slipped back two steps.'
'Well, how did you get to school then?' asked
the puzzled teacher.
'Well, I gave up trying to get to school and
went home!'

# The Name Game

If Santa climbs down the chimney, who climbs up it?

IVY

La la la

What do you call a girl who likes to sing at Christmas?

CAROL

Who wants a do-it-yourself kit?

ANDY

Who gets underpants for Christmas?

NICHOLAS

Who pays for all the presents?

BILL

cough! Yuk!

Who's going to be given
cigarettes for Christmas?

**NICK O'TEEN**

Who's got a cold and needs
some chest ointment?

**VIC**

Who crashed his new bike
on Boxing Day?

**REX**

Who would you give
a telescope to?

**SEYMOUR**

Who's that buried under
the wrapping paper?

**RUSSELL**

# CRACKER

How do you stop a dog from barking
in the back of a car?
*Put him in the front.*

Which king was a chiropodist?
*William the Corn Curer!*

Where does Tarzan get his clothes from?
*A jungle sale.*

What's green and swings through the jungle?
*A septic monkey.*

...at happened to the monster that ate
...clear power station?
...ot atomic ache.

# JOKES

What's yellow and swings through the jungle going, 'Ahee ahee ahh'?
*Tarzipan!*

Why did the Romans build straight roads?
*So that the Ancient Britons couldn't hide round the corners.*

Why does a stork stand on one foot?
*Because if he lifted the other one he'd fall over.*

Doctor, doctor, I think I'm a dog.
*Well, sit down on the couch and tell me about it.*
But I'm not allowed on the furniture!

If a buttercup is yellow, what colour is a hiccup?
*Burple.*

'SCUSE ME!

# Pet Jokes

Just to be serious a moment, a lot of people are given pets at Christmas. If you are one of them, remember that they need lots of love and feeding every day, all the year round. You can't just get rid of them on Boxing Day, if you get bored with them. However, pets are a whole load of fun. So, on with the jokes!

We got an octopuss last Christmas . . .
It was an eight-sided cat.

I got a five-pound note for Christmas but the cat ate it.
*Never mind, it's always good to keep something in the kitty.*

Our cat ate a ball of wool . . .
Now she's having mittens.

Our kitten thinks he's a motor bike . . .
He goes down the motorway going
Meeeeeeeeeeeeeeeow!

I gave our cat something to sleep on
for Christmas . . . it was a caterpillow.

We were going to buy Gran a kitten for
Christmas. Dad asked the man in the shop if
they had any going cheap.
'No, sir,' replied the shopkeeper, 'all our
kittens go meow.'

Why is Christmas like a cat at the seaside?
*They both have sandy claws.*

We got a dog for Christmas that can speak a foreign language.

We got a miniature poodle for Christmas . . .
The minute you turn your back
he poodles on the carpet.

Our dog's got ticks.
*Well, don't wind him up then.*

How do you get an elephant
into a Christmas cracker?
*Take out the party hat first.*

There's an owl nesting in
the barn. You can tell
that he's not interested
in Christmas . . .
He couldn't give a hoot.

Who does give a hoot?

I had to share a bed with
an elephant last night.

How did you know
it was an elephant?

Well, when he hung up
his stocking it had
a great big E
embroidered on it.

What's the difference between a penguin
and an elephant?
*You can't get the wrapper off an elephant.*

Why not
a puffin?

Jim got a goldfish for Christmas. On twelfth
night Mum said it should have its water
changed.

But Mum, he hasn't drunk
the last lot yet!

What did the bull say after he'd been
Christmas shopping in a china shop?
*'I've had a smashing time.'*

What do monkeys sing at Christmas time?
Jungle bells
Jungle bells
Jungle all the way!

# Postman's Knock

Uncle Clive once did a holiday job
as a postman. The first thing
they did was to give him the sack!

Do you know the difference between an elephant and a letter-box?

No.

Well, that's the last time I ask you to post my Christmas cards!

# CRACKER

Have you heard about the golfer who always has a spare pair of trousers with him?
*It's in case he gets a hole in one.*

What did the first tonsil say to the second tonsil?
*The doctor is taking me out tonight.*

What do you call a cat that's just eaten a duck?
*A duck-filled fatty puss!*

What's yellow and smells of bananas?
*Monkey sick.*

What is white on the outside, green on the inside and goes ribbet, ribbet?
*A frog sandwich.*

RIBBET!

# JOKES

Have you heard about the football team that have never met each other?
*They're called Queens Park Strangers.*

Where does a general keep his army?
*Up his sleevy.*

What is the most dangerous fish in the sea?
*Jack the Kipper!*

How do you start a teddy bear's picnic?
*Ready, teddy, go!*

What's white and fluffy and lives in tr
*A meringue utan!*

# While Shepherds Washed Their Socks

What is the best way to make money when you go carol singing?
*Go to all the people who will pay you to go away.*

I'm going carol singing.

What, with a dirty face?

No, with Jim next door.

While shepherds washed their socks by night,
all seated round the tub,
a bar of Sunlight soap came down
and they began to scrub!

What letters were the Three Wise Men
carrying?
*Ys of course!*

There was this bellringer
who kept forgetting to
let go of the rope . . .
He wanted to go up
in the world.

What do you find in the
farmyard that sounds
like bells?
*DUNG!*

What did one bellringer
say to the other?

How's dings with you?

What do you get if you eat
Christmas decorations?
*Tinselitis!*

What's going to happen at Christmas?
*Yule have a great time.*

Why is a Christmas tree like a clumsy tailor?
*Because they both drop their needles.*

What's wrong with writing a letter to Santa?
*You shouldn't put all your begs in one ask it.*

I can think of better ways to spend Christmas.

Why will the television never take the place of newspapers over Christmas?
*Have you ever tried to swat a fly with a television?*

Do you know we only switched the telly on once over Christmas? We thought we'd better turn it off on New Year's Day though!

Would you like a Christmas surprise?

How can I make you laugh on Boxing Day?
I'll tell you a joke on Christmas Day.

Why is December one of the warmest months
of the year?
*Because it has embers in it.*

We always burn candles at Christmas but
have you seen the price of candles this year?
It's candelous!

What did the big cracker
say to the little cracker?

# Knock Knock

Knock, knock.
*Who's there?*
Fozzie.
*Fozzie who?*
Fozzie hundredth
time, will you
open the door?

Knock, knock.
*Who's there?*
Theodore.
*Theodore who?*
Theodore is shut
and you haven't
got a chimney.

Knock, knock.
*Who's there?*
Sssssss.
*Sssssss who?*
Sssssstttop
mucking about,
it's cold out
here.

Knock, knock.
*Who's there?*
Andrew.
*Andrew who?*
Andrew the
curtains so I
couldn't see
if you were in.

I'm still cold!

Knock, knock.
*Who's there?*
Police.
*Police who?*
Police let me
in, it's cold
out here!

Knock, knock.
*Who's there?*
Justin.
*Justin who?*
Justin time
to deliver
the presents.

Knock, knock.
*Who's there?*
Trish.
*Trish who?*
Oh dear, I didn't
know you had
a cold.

Knock, knock.
*Who's there?*
Cook.
*Cook who?*
Who ever heard
of a cuckoo
at Christmas.

Knock, knock.
*Who's there?*
Phyllis.
*Phyllis who?*
Phyllis a bucket
of water, the
door's on fire.

Knock, knock.
*Who's there?*
Jester.
*Jester who?*
Jester minute,
I'll unlock
the door.

# CRACKER

Do you know that if it wasn't for railway timetables we wouldn't know that the trains were running late.

How do you get a milkshake?
*Give a cow a pogo stick.*

What do you get if you cross a sheep with a kangaroo?
*A woolly jumper with pockets in it.*

How can a mountain hear things?
*It uses its mountainears.*

at do frogs drink?
*aka-Cola!*

BURP!

# JOKES

Do you know what's green, slimy, has
ninety-nine legs and vicious-looking teeth?
Well, there's one crawling up your neck.

Your skin is like a peach . . .
A football peach!

Why do moths eat less than anything else?
*Because they only eat holes.*

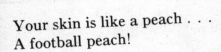

How do you open a door in a Turkish house?
*Use a turkey.*

What's tall and wobbles in the middle of
Paris?
*The Trifle Tower!*

# Relative Values

'We always phone our relatives at
Christmas.'
*'That must cost a lot.'*
'Not really, we wait until they aren't at
home!'

How do you make anti-freeze?
*Put her in the fridge.*

Mum asked Jim to get some cream
for the mince pies.
'Single or double?' asked the milkman.
'Oh! Just a small one,' said Jim.

A friend of Jim's never said a word from
when he was a baby until he was seven years
old when, during Christmas dinner, he
suddenly said,
'I don't think much of the Christmas
pudding!'
His parents were overjoyed to hear him
speak after so long and asked him why he
had never spoken before.
'Well,' said the boy, 'everything has been OK
up until now!'

'Mum is having a new baby for Christmas.'
*'Why, what's wrong with the last one?'*

Uncle Clive snores so loudly that he wakes
himself up.
He's all right now – he sleeps in another
room!

'Granny, have you lived here all your life?'
*'Not yet, son, not yet.'*

'Dad was doing pop art on Christmas Day.'
*'I didn't know he was an artist.'*
'He's not. He had to pop art down the pub
for a quick pint!'

Uncle Clive caught fire on Christmas
Day . . .
He was wearing his new blazer!

'Tina, why did you put a spider
in your auntie's bed?'
*'Because Dad couldn't find a frog!'*

Our auntie is a cross-eyed teacher . . .
She can't control her pupils.

Your auntie reminds me of a film star . . .
Lassie!

'So, your auntie brings happiness
wherever she goes?'
*'No, I said WHENever she goes!'*

'Dad lost his temper on Christmas Day.'
*'Oh, but that's awful.'*
'Not really, it was a bad one anyway.'

'My gran has got a glass eye.'
*'How did you find that out?'*
'Oh, it came out in conversation!'

When we all left Grannie's on Christmas
Day, she gave Uncle Clive a parting gift . . .
it was a comb!

Gran's house is always freezing at Christmas.
I asked her if there was any chance of us
having a fire. She said no, she always keeps
a bucket of water handy.

Granny was the toast of the town last
Christmas . . .
She forgot to turn off her electric blanket!

'How are you getting on at school, Tina?'
*'Not very well, Gran,*
*I've got to go back again next term!'*

Read it! Read it!

Big Bang! DINAH MIGHT

HAVE A GOOD TRIP · Mister Step

The long goodbye - C.U. Later

Pebbles on the beach ∘ Sandy Shore

JAILBREAK ∘ FREDA PRISONER

Lunchtime snacks - Roland Butter

Bubbles in the bath : Ivor Windybottom

Twit!

WHAT'S FOR TEA?
M. T. TUM-TUM

Take your Punishment— Ben Dover

The incredible Journey: Ellen Back

ADVERTISING BILL STICKERS

HAUNTED HOUSES. I.Malone & I.M.Scared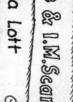

The Disappearing Turkey — Henrietta Lott

Christmas Recipies — E.Titup

Nothing but the truth — Liza Lott

Cliffhanger —
illustrated by Betty Wont
WILLY MAYKIT

Twenty Years in the Saddle — Major Bumsore

BELL RINGING — PAULA ROPE

Silent Night — Carol Singer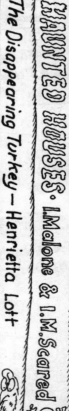

# CRACKER

What does an X-ray of your brain show?
*Not much!*

I used to be a werewolf
but I'm all right now-ow-owwwww!

Did you hear about the human cannon-ball?
*He got fired!*

Why can't a train sit down?
*Because it has a tender behind.*

invented the five-day week?
inson Crusoe, because he had all of his
k done by Friday.

# JOKES

Why did the little girl take her crayons to bed with her?
*Because she wanted to draw the curtains.*

What do you call two rows of cabbages?
*A dual cabbage way.*

What do hippies do?
*They hold your leggies on.*

How can you tell how heavy a whale is?
*Take it to a whale weigh station.*

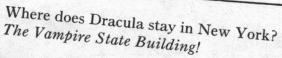

Where does Dracula stay in New York?
*The Vampire State Building!*

# Gobblers!

Why did the turkey cross the road?
*To prove he wasn't chicken.*

YOUNG TURKEY: Hello, Mum, I've brought a friend home for Christmas dinner.
MUM: *But it's only September, dear.*
YOUNG TURKEY: That's all right, we can keep him in the deep freeze!

Why did the turkey fall in love with the chicken?
*Because she egged him on a bit.*

All the young turkeys went to a Christmas dance . . .
They danced chick to chick.

Mummy, I hate Daddy's guts.
*Well, leave them on the side of the plate,
dear!*

FIRST TURKEY:  We had our relations for
Christmas.
SECOND TURKEY:  *That's tough.*
FIRST TURKEY:  I know,
chicken is a lot more tender.

There was a turkey who rubbed oil under his
wings on Christmas Eve . . .
He wanted to get up oily on Christmas Day.

Why did the young turkey rush his dinner?
*Because he was a little gobbler.*

Where do good turkeys go to when they die?
*They go to oven.*

If Dad could see you now
he'd turn in his gravy.

'How much are your turkeys?'
'70p a pound, madam.'
'Did you raise them yourself?'
*'Yes, madam, they were only 50p
a pound this morning!'*

Why do we pluck the feathers off the turkey?
*No one likes to feel down in the mouth on
Christmas Day.*

Why is a turkey like a harp?
*Because they both have to be plucked.*

Young turkey eating his Christmas lunch:
'Mum, I don't like Dad.'
*'Well, eat your potatoes instead!'*

Why is a turkey like a sofa?
*They're both full of stuffing.*

There was once a turkey farmer who thought
that since everyone likes a turkey leg, he
would breed three-legged turkeys.
He was very successful but they ran so fast
that he couldn't catch them.

# GHOST STORY

'We've got a ghost that walks through the house on Christmas Eve.'
*'How does it get in the house?'*
'It uses skeleton keys!'

Your money or your life!

Take my life . . . I'm saving up for Christmas!

What do you give a houseproud ghost for Christmas?
*An Oooooooooooooooover!*

OOOOOOH!

What is special about a Christmas carol that
is sung by a ghost?
*It has a haunting melody.*

Did you hear about the ghost who gave his
wife a girdle for Christmas so that she could
keep her ghoulish figure?

Where do monsters get their
Christmas presents from?
*Santa Claws.*

Where do sea monsters get their
Christmas presents from?
*Santa Jaws.*

# CRACKER

Oh yes, God uses our bathroom you know.
Every morning Dad bangs on the bathroom
door and says,
'Oh God, are you still in there?'

What sits in a fruit bowl and screams?
*A damson in distress.*

My darling, you are like a peach . . .
You have a heart of stone.

What do you call a bald bear?
*Fred bear.*

How did the Vikings send messages?
*Norse code.*

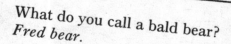

# JOKES

My dad thinks he's a chicken. The doctor said that he could cure him but we need the eggs!

What has four legs and flies?
*A dead horse.*

Why did the shrimp blush?
*Because it saw the* Queen Mary's *bottom.*

Your feet are like petals . . .
Bicycle petals.

Why did the lobster blush?
*Because it saw the salad dressing.*

# Doctor Doctor!

The doctor says that
Dad has water on the
knee, so we're going
to give him some
drainpipe trousers
for Christmas.

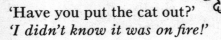

'Have you put the cat out?'
*'I didn't know it was on fire!'*

'Did you have a nice Christmas?'
*'No, I swallowed a roll of film.*
*The doctor is waiting for something to*
*develop.'*

Dad ate so much over Christmas that he got
horribly ill. After the doctor had left
he looked really worried.
The doctor said that he would have to take
pills for the rest of his life. The problem is
that he only gave Dad four!

Did you hear about the bunny rabbit that
was ill at a Christmas party?
*He mixed his toasties.*

After all the food that Dad ate at Christmas
he thought he should diet, but he couldn't
decide on a colour!

Did you hear about the man who went bang
on Christmas Day?
*He was crackers.*

You won't be able
to eat any cake
after that lot,
will you?

Of course not . . .
I am on a diet,
you know!

# Stocking Fillers

Who hides in a bakery at Christmas?
*A mince spy.*

What nationality is Santa?
*North Polish.*

Why does Santa sit the wrong way on his sleigh?
*Because he knows the Highway Code backwards.*

Why did Santa fly over the mountain?
*Because he couldn't fly through it.*

'I was given a cake for Christmas.
It was horrible.'
*'But I thought you liked cake.'*
'I do, but it was a cake of soap!'

Tina went to the loo in the middle of the
pantomime. When she came back there was
an enormous man sitting in her seat.
'Excuse me, that's my seat,' whispered Tina.
'Prove it!' rasped the man.
'Well, I think you'll find I left
my ice-cream on it!'

Jim was the last to leave Tina's Christmas party. He couldn't find his boots anywhere.
'Here they are,' said Tina's mum.
'Those aren't mine,' said Jim, 'mine had snow on them.'

We gave Gran a foolproof gadget for the kitchen.
Of course she couldn't get it to work!

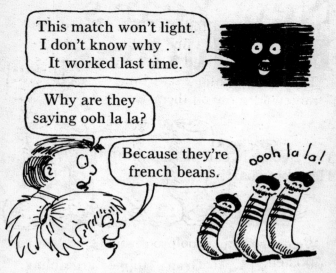

This match won't light.
I don't know why . . .
It worked last time.

Why are they
saying ooh la la?

Because they're
french beans.

oooh la la!

Jim was searching round the house for one of
his Christmas presents.
'Mum,' he called out, 'I've lost my marbles.'
'Well, I know you're a bit stupid, son,' said
Mum, 'but I wouldn't say you were that far
gone!'

Mum, you know that really
expensive pen you gave me?
Well, it's run out.

Well, you'd bet
run after it an
catch it then

# New Year's Resolutions

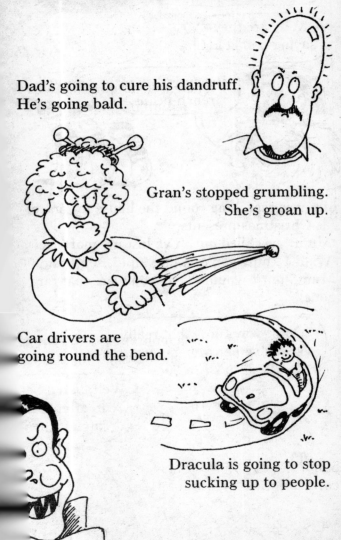

Dad's going to cure his dandruff.
He's going bald.

Gran's stopped grumbling.
She's groan up.

Car drivers are
going round the bend.

Dracula is going to stop
sucking up to people.

Barney the sheep is going to
the baah baahs for a hair cut.

The gardener is going to be
led up the garden path.

Nudists are going to appear
to have nothing on.

The demolition man is going
to have a smashing time.

Santa is going to weed his
garden with his Hoe Hoe Hoe.

# Left-over Pudding

Something to keep you busy on Boxing Day. You will need:

1. The remains of the turkey.
2. 2 lbs of all the stuff that hides at the back of the fridge.
3. 8 packets of raisins. (Rabbit droppings will do if you got a bunny for Christmas!)
4. Last year's Christmas pudding that you didn't get round to eating.
5. All the walnuts that are too tough to open.
6. All the needles that have dropped off the Christmas tree (and anything else that got sucked up in the Hoover at the same time).
7. All the hard-centred chocolates that Granny only managed to suck the chocolate off.

# What To Do

If Mum got a brand-new food processor or
mixer for Christmas, use it. (It's under
guarantee.)
Break open last year's Christmas pudding.
(If Dad got a brand-new hammer action
drill, use it!)
Use the turkey roasting tin. If no one has
done the washing up it should be really
messy. Shovel the mixture into the tin. Bake
for three days at 100°F.
When it's ready, if I were you, I'd bung it
down the loo, pull the chain and say good
riddance!

Merry Christmas and a Happy New Year

Shoo Rayner